To Mari
With Best

Yoik

B.b B.... 24-1-08

BOB BEAGRIE

Cinnamon Press
Independent Innovative International

Published by Cinnamon Press
Meirion House, Glan yr afon, Tanygrisiau, Blaenau Ffestiniog,
Gwynedd LL41 3SU www.cinnamonpress.com

The right of Bob Beagrie to be identified as author of this work has
been asserted by him in accordance with the Copyright, Designs and
Patent Act, 1988. © 2008 Bob Beagrie ISBN 978-1-905614-40-0
British Library Cataloguing in Publication Data. A CIP record for this
book can be obtained from the British Library.
Designed and typeset in Palatino by Cinnamon Press
Cover design by Mike Fortune-Wood from original artwork by Robert
Smith © Robert Smith
The publisher acknowledges the financial support of the Welsh Books
Council.

Acknowledgements

Some of the poems have appeared in the following magazines,
anthologies and pamphlets: *Fire, Other Poetry, Sand, Interpoetry,
Dreamcatcher, Next Stop Hope* (Route), *The Flesh of the Bear* (Ek Zuban),
Smelter (Mudfog), *Magnetic North* (New Writing North), *Miracle &
Clockwork* (Other Poetry Editions), *North by North East* (Iron Press),
Tadeeb International, Perkele (Ek Zuban) and *The Wilds* (Ek Zuban).

Hugh MacDiarmid's 'Island Funeral' was first published in *The
Islands of Scotland: Hebrides, Orkneys, Shetlands*. London: B.T. Batsford,
1939. The quote is taken from *Selected Poetry*, Carcanet (1992) and is
used with kind permission of Carcanet Press Ltd. The quote from
Christopher Lasch is taken from *The Culture of Narcissism: American
Life in an Age of Diminishing Expectations*, p.51, W.W Norton. (1979)
with kind permission. The epigraph is from Jorge Luis Borge, 'The
Preface to The Unending Rose', translated by Alastair Reid *The Book
of Sand*, Penguin (1989) by kind permission of Pollinger Ltd.

Thanks go to Andy Willoughby for fanning the flames. Also many
thanks to Jo Colley, Kalle Niinikangas and Esa Hirvonen and to Kate
Rider for the guiding hand through Steers.

Notes:

Yoik is an original form of Sami music, and an integral part of the ancient religion of Shamanism. You don't yoik about someone, something or someplace, but rather yoik something, someone or someplace. Having one's own yoik was once as important as having a name. Yoik was always used – along with the drum – by the noaide to provoke the trance that would be necessary for the ritual.

Domestic: Based one of the Baltic Dainas. The Dainas are unique Latvian folksongs in verse form, covering all aspects of ancient Baltic life, mythology and astronomy. Saule is the sun goddess who rides her steeds to the Island of Apples each day. Menes, the moon god, is her jealous husband.

Lovi: Ancient Finnish term which denotes the hole through which a noaide (shaman) will fall as he/she enters the underworld in the form of a trance vision. In modern Finnish Lovi means love. Vainomoinen is a tragic, warrior-wizard hero from the Finnish epic poem *The Kalevela*.

With The Knowledge of the Birds: Poem based on the Cheyenne myth of the same name.

The Bard: An overdraft of Thomas Gray's *The Bard*: a Pindaric Ode, which inspired the John Martin painting *The Bard* (1817). It recounts the tale of the last Welsh Warrior Bard, hunted down by Edward I.

The Gift & Like the Last Bard: Contemporary interpretations of the painting *The Bard*, in The Laing Gallery, Newcastle upon Tyne.

The Great Entertainer: Based on the Great Storm of February 1861, in which eighty ships where seriously damaged in Hartlepool and the sinking of the Rising Sun. (The Great Entertainer and Ritual, were written during a residency on The Hartlepool Headland, 2005.)

Pililu: Old Gaelic lament based on the call of the red shank.

Contents

Periphrastics:

The Bard:

Suomi & Other Yoiking Locations:

to Louise for ever and always

The mission of the poet should be to restore to the
word, at least in a partial way, its primitive and now
secret force. All verse should have two obligations: to
communicate a precise instance and to touch us
physically, as the presence of the sea does.

Jorge Luis Borges
Preface to *The Unending Rose*

Yoik

Periphrastics

Statement of Intent

I scrawl when the subtext of TV sets ma teeth on edge.
Draft the cliff's retreat as waves break to bubbles
on rock rubble, on sand, n' those bubbles burst to nothing.

Scratch words that hover-static as a hawk on the verge
of the A19; balanced on a high-wind above a hedgerow
    –   once a forest, wide beyond thought.

I scribble the traffic's stream of chatter
wi' all its impatience to be any place but here.

Spell stammerwort's conversations in brookbabble,
in rainfall, in wild garlic clouds of undergreen folds
    – thru pleats between roads.

One day I'll write the kestrel's eyes,
locked on the movement of a meaning
creeping live n' hot thru the hedge.

The Linesman

This morning's so primed for living
or dying, you must remember to wear
a Superman top under your shirt;
for you met, last night, a man named Lorry
The brother of a friend's ex-girlfriend,
who was once a driver in the army
and always went on the sick
rather than go to war with the nifty trick
of popping his hip joint out of its socket.
Saw his mates come back damaged, not fit
for anything anymore. So when he left
he became a linesman, climbing pylons,

Been electrocuted dozens of times,
As long as you're not grounded you can handle it
it's the best job in the world, up there
in the Outer Hebrides, in all weathers
in France, on the west coast of Ireland
where on a clear day you can almost spot America
and all hangovers are shed on the climb
and the money's great and there's travel,
good crack and lots of fine women
and I've fallen dozens of times in the past,
Mostly I've bounced, but last time
I landed on concrete and broke both my legs.
Doctors said I'd never walk again,
but eighteen months later I'm walking fine.
I could have sued, but I'd never work again.
I've tortured myself in the gym
and snapped a steel pin in one leg

but eighteen months later – I'm walking fine
and waiting for a doctor to sign the form
that says I can go back to work, get back there
cos it's the best job there is, among the lines,
and when you've climbed through the frosty web
to see the sunrise, you're the king of the world.

Snake Eye

*Narcissism appears realistically to represent the best way of coping with
the tensions and anxieties of ultramodern life.*

Christopher Lasch. The Culture of Narcissism.

Two nights of fever dreams in the humidity
of August, legs tying themselves in the sheets.
Two sandwiched days of shuffling like I'm forty years
older than my years. Retinas burning winces
from deep aches and surface spasms. It came on
like a cobra-bite, started with a cold shiver
till it felt as if someone had stabbed my left eye.
I took a few days off to crawl inside my shell.
Batten down the hatches to wait out the worst of it.
Spend some quality time with my old ghosts,
and new ones, with their deadline deliriums,
their forked impossibilities flick-sniffing me out.

The second night the pain grew blunt, but spread
behind my cheek and jaw. The snakes were back.
Slithering thru the creaks of the hot house, thru the pipes,
and the marrow of it. Spitting phone calls not made,
e's not returned, letters unwritten, reports, arrangements,
expectations not met. All I wanted was to strip off my face,
burn my name, shed the constrictions of my skin.
Wondering what's going on? What on earth have I seen?

Was it that wasp-sting in the eye from a few months back?
Maybe, it didn't just sting, but laid some eggs as well
and they've hatched to start devouring my brain!
Or maybe my best mate, who I cut short last week,
has since crafted a doll around a hair I left, inadvertently,
on his carpet and is slowly working his needles.
Or else it's Wisdom arriving in my mouth – that seems
a little far fetched, but on Nights of the Snake, you rule
nothing out. I'm prone to these crashes once in a while.

It was bright again by the time sleep came. But today
I was more my usual shape, though less prone to movement.
filled-up by the sunshine on the water, the water-light's
shimmer on the underside of the bridge. Well gifted,
as we drifted on the river, ate ice cream by the cathedral.
Paid our respects to Cuthbert, felt unusually comfortable
with Slow. While The Nights of the Snake have slid
into my back-brain drawer, leaving a twinge in my kidneys
one nostril refusing to work. But that's nowt –
Why! Tomorrow I'll be fit enough to turn cartwheels
down the hillside, heading straight for white water
staring wild and stopping short before the rocks.

Storm Damage

The rest of the country is baking
(the hottest day in 130 years)
but within half an hour
our summer glow's stubbed out
like a half-smoked cigar.

The dark is not like night.
More like coal dust on the wind
like an eclipse
like someone's killed the son of god
then thunder
close; as the Atlantic lands and bounces.

Looking out of the window it's like we're under water.

Already, sirens are whining.
The roofs and seals are bursting.
Leaks blossom in the plasterwork
and any dry towel is a god-send.

Shoppers are swimming in Morrisons,
and Binns; Barker & Stonehouse
will hold a flood-damaged sale.

Once the torrent has rolled out to sea to drown
we go for a drive through steam ravaged trees,
the symphony of drips, and can't find any way out of town.

Every route's eventually blocked by fire engines,
kids wading up to their waists, paddling across to Grannies
on doors they'd been hoarding for the bommie.

A dodgy punter who likes it rough, with a license plate
from Leeds is marooned in the Zone for the night.
And at Brambles Farm a bloke with tread-lines
running through his wet-gelled hair
balances on a bollard above the water line
red in the face and bellowing at the tower blocks

Leave me wife and me kids alone.
Get it straight, its over, yeh hear. Its over!

Domestic

From the Baltic Dainas

1

His pasty flesh on her carving knife
like lumps of half baked bread.

All those princely looks scattered
to the wind, like his crime, willy-nilly.

His teeth she cast like seed
from the back of her golden Porsche

and if, in a month of Sundays,
I managed to pull him together

she'd want a divorce.

Though she'd help any lost lamb
she still simmers in rage.

Though she'd ride the sky to bring us light
she can't bare the sound of his name.

Nor listen to excuses.
Nor tolerate talk of his rehabilitation,

He's streaked with deep seated jealousy.

My mother is wild and sleeps in the Big Apple.
Been spotted on benches in Central Park,

snapped riding the Ghost Train on Coney Island
before swimming back to the East.

2

Menes once wore a cloak of stars,
used to ride by her side through the land

over the sea, on his days off, in all weathers
till the night of the storm

when he found one light-giver gone.
Where's Auskilis on a night like this?

Germany, making money.
Gone to make a packet of bread.

But he thought he knew they were lying.
That Morning Star is screwing my wife!

Menes plucked me like a hair from my bed
all scowls and pearly teeth

gagged me with tape, bound my hands tight
pulled a blindfold over my eyes

but what the light-givers saw the light-givers told
and Saule took hold of her carving knife

and snipped the rope and the fold and the tape
and sliced my stepfather Menes to slivers

and once she'd stormed away
to sleep off her rage on the Island of Apples

I took pity on his remains, collected his fingers,
his buttocks, his ribs, his head and penis

and I pieced him together to make a marquette
Of a man-in-the-moon on a backdrop of sky.

Cuchulain's Lullaby

on double time, cash in hand

Snort, burlesque bull-bouncer
low on Exchange Square,
scanning herds in wattage orange

the valley's folded Christmas zeal
pours Nativity scenes from garage mouths

all the streets, gritted roads
brittle avenues n' frosted groves
fight n' race for grottodom
to be the first He'll visit

ah promise yeh

without a doubt, the doormen tap-dance
sly with segs, slide n' shuffle, soak up stares
like buffalo mounds in freezing fog

hulking shadows, black on grey
around megaliths, worn tumuli
knee-high bollards n' thin black ice

blart n' bother clinging tight
copping slurred snogs n' covert gropes
underneath the Green Man's bleep

early doors

the queues are safe in the crack
of a 22 carat tooth, ironed out
by a bleached blonde stare

six pupils swimming in each eye
six irises like jade tigers dancing the jitter
of Redbull, tuned-in to the overflow
of mood n' booze n' powdered highs

says yeh then nah, in green, in red
nods 'em in then holds 'em back

no fuss

this hound will smile polite
to' suss the yabber
even take a pinch of raw faced cheek

he cooks his paws
in white vinegar n' herbs, trained 'em
to kill with a simple tap

his bark has become rose quartz
spends the days carving edges
marking points in shifting maps

last orders

waits like a nail bomb for some tanked
-up bloke who's out to prove
a bitter point n' knows a few good moves

the hound is wired n' licensed to warp
the night back into shape, diffuse
the situation with a raised full glove

n' lead with his nut in a cold tamed rage
to gore with receded horns n' guard
the rites of Yuletide's turn

in dark dawn

after a parmo, a sleet squall drives
Cuchulain home, inch by inch
he scrubs the night scents from his pores

before sneaking-in
between warm sheets to spoon
his body about Nemain's sleep.

Upon Waking

For Florence Beagrie

All night Death prowled around her house
sang through the letterbox, tapped on the window pane
tugged at her weeping legs, and the news that He
had taken Rosie in March filled the corridors
of her broken sleep; but Florrie had sent him packing
often enough, tail tucked between His legs, His ear thick
from a clout from the back of her hand. And when
the glimmer of life and pain spread through her frame
and she opened the lid of her one good eye, her house
was full of people pretending to be real: the carers,
the district nurse, the neighbour, the grand daughter-in-law.
What in hell's going on? I'm not going to hospital again!
She knows full well He is stronger than her in there.
How He wanders through the wards at will.

With the Knowledge of the Birds

It's true, I once lived with the hawk,
though I sharpened my words
in place of a beak,
though I fashioned a flint knife
as I lacked the talons,
but flew on their backs, holding tight
round their necks, over the treetops
and blinding light lakes.

Wrapped in a cloak of second-hand feathers
I slept in a nest in their cave
with my hawk husband, hawk father
my hawk grandfather with his one blind eye,
who tucked me under their wing.

Singed, forever sooty once we'd killed the old owl,
who would have torn me apart like a shrew,
and burnt his body on the hillside each Spring.

Flames sizzled all over his feathers
and precious things tumble out:
crystals, wishes, promises, curses.
Don't touch them, said Grandfather,
Poke them into the embers with a stick.

So I did, though the desire to gather
was almost too much to bare,
like spotting the moon in the dew of a cobweb,
like a mother at the end of her tether –
who'd throw a brat-child out into the night,
spitting, *There, have it your way.*
Let the owls take you, if they want you.

3 Little Piggies

After a night shift guarding a quarter of a million cigs
Roy calls round to ours to smoke a few
with a sweet cup of tea and to wind-up the girl
with a fossil in her pocket. Sun on magnolia.
Bonsai's bud-popping their first slivers of leaves.
She wants a picnic. Lays out doll's plates, a yellow teapot.
Sets about sharing our rations; plastic sausages
a hollow baguette. Three plastercine plums.
You can sit here Roy. Just there. Pointing
to the spot by the house spider's hole.
All three of us tuck in, nibbling like rabbits into the edge
of a brand new summer. Then she says she's sad
Doesn't want to be all of 4. Wants to be 3 3/4 forever.
I catch Roy's eye, say nowt, knowing he knows the feeling.

Brink

For Robyn

And don't fear the shade
for it will protect you
from the high glare,
from predatory eyes,
until you are ready
to emerge in your own
good time and spread
your wings wide;
notice how shade
will shift as all shade does;
and pay attention
to the peripheries
for it's there that change
first registers,
become accustomed
to the spread of the blur
with the breath
settling like dusk,
and accept
with good heart
your own peripheral nature
as a sanctuary on the palm
of your god.

The Bard

The Bard

I.1. Strophe

All day we've ridden through the hills
In rain and cold, through patches of sun
That broke through holes in the outer frills
Of clouds that let their shadows run,
Headstrong from the peaks like the charging ranks
Of revolt to the hammer of Edward Longshanks.
We War Dogs clank as our horses plod
From woodland caves forsaken by God
To deserted villages, past barren fields
Our bright helms, hauberks, our riding shields
Hang heavy this eve, my eyes play tricks
The trees whistle hate from a Welsh wind's kicks
Where an outlaw poet speaks an ancient tongue
Cambria's curse, that wrong will follow wrong.

I.2. Antistrophe

Put them all to death. Our orders from the crown
Strangle their songs of resistance, one by one!
I have seen some burn, I have seen some drown.
Only once did I ask, *Lord, what have we done?*
When one I skewered upon mine own lance
Who continued to sing, as I in speechless trance
Watched his bloodied lips begin to weave the woof
Weave the warp, as he died upon my sharpened tooth.
But one native bard remains within the land
To cry the renegades' mournful tune,
A grisly band sworn to fight, to die at his command
Their hands as crimson as my helmet's plume.
Who would willingly rip themselves asunder
Madmen or fools, we have no time to ponder?

I.3. Epode

My sovereign would be Overlord of all the Isles,
From the towers of Julius, his castle courts
To Caledonia beyond the Roman wall.
From these wild lands of barbarous hordes
Once quelled, we'll smite the Tir na nÓg
Across Hibernia, Edward's name we'll scrawl
With swords as quills on the men of the bog.
As we've done here on dreary Arvon's shore
Ghastly pale and smeared with gore.
Llewellyn's forces lie cold in silence
Save for the ghosts of the last Bard's companions;
Pockets of insurgents hidden in the mountains.
Our hounds race baying before our stallions.
This night we'll skin our quarry's remains
They have his scent. This way he went
Little more than an hour past,
Crossed these falls. Up he's crawled
To yonder cliffs to stand aghast
Like a prize stag of seven tines, a lone oak tree
On a broken crag overlooking tumbling Conwy.

II.1. Strophe

His hair a swallow-tailed, frosted pennant
His prophet's beard, a Gwynedd blizzard.
Instead of fleeing, he tears a chord of pure lament
From his lyre – the next a note of disregard
For this wretched life. It cuts through mail.
As we ride up the track he begins to wail
An echo up through Snowdon's heights,
Come pirate King and thy chivalrous knights
Come and face thy fate, as I face mine.
Thine ambition will lead thee to the gates of hell
So sup my sweet nation's blood like wine.
Thine chronicles will read what Time will tell,
Thine own Empire will drown in a sea of blood,
Thine heir will undo all that you deem good.

11.2. Antistrophe

Our fugitive's words are elemental
Vulgar, as raw as a lightening bolt.
Each syllable a blacksmith's hammer on metal
Each vowel a wound dowsed in salt.
Not a poet laureate to entertain the court
Or flatter Princelings with fine phrases wrought
Like bejewelled goblets from an Eastern shore
Brought back as curios for Queen Eleanor,
Some fancy pilfered during the ninth crusade,
Smuggled back to England with the secret of glass.
No, this druid's prayers ring with a torrent's rage
Coarse as a moorland campfire, black as burnt grass.
His venomous tirade rides a swarm of plague rats
That wreath like smoke down the mountain track.

II.3. Epode

Forward! To arms! Mortimer cries,
Over the din of this bard's feral verses,
Onward! He has nowhere else to climb.
Who'll put an end to his vile curses?
Who'll tear out his tongue? Bring me his hide!
Sew up his lips, butcher his rhyme!
Tonight we bury their tales, their hoary propaganda
Tonight we craft a new story to hail
Of an English Prince of Wales!
And yet I half suspect our wild charge a blunder.
The booming voice – enough to freeze our lugs,
Turn them blue, and open the gates to Annwn.
Fearing an ambush from his faery thugs
Along the ridges, a well aimed rock in a sling
From our fallen foes, a sudden rain of arrows
Let loose from sorrow's tether, but ours
Is not to reason why, but to ride – to ride
And meet Doom with a fixed grin.
Sir Mortimer leads our gleaming array
With horns resounding for his Historic day.

III.1. Strophe

But no assault from hand or sling or bow
Descends from Snowdon's shaggy slopes,
But above the gorge a bedraggled crow
Takes to thin air like the bard's last hope.
And we surmise this man to be alone,
Singing a mantra that makes the mountain groan –
For the final remnant of a guerrilla war.
Dismounting, I race up the screed-covered floor
Drawing my sword to end our just and noble cause.
Placing our actions against the code of chivalry
Many of our company obey an urge to pause,
Questioning for a moment the extent of misery
That will follow our lives like a grim shadow.
His prophecies hold the chill of a hallowed barrow.

III.2. Antistrophe

Come to me, my boy, the old boar calls,
Let me weave your warp, your thread I'll spin!
Inching ever closer, over gnarled rocks I crawl,
Know me better, man! He claims the name Taliesin.
I was the child once known as Gwion,
Who supped the broth brewed by the witch Ceridwen.
And since that day I can become all things,
From the snows of the high passes to a hornet's sting.
And you think your sword will put an end to my tune?
You think to claim my head for your tyrant King?
If you grind down my bones I'll return like the moon.
Sword in my right hand, my left a mace begins to swing.
And he in a black robe, and unarmed but for his lyre
Laughs as he plays – a cackle that scorches like fire.

III.3. Epode

Finish this! brave Mortimer yells from below,
The day has come and gone, the night heralds snow.
But what dread truths I'm told as I circle the rock,
Things of a future I'd rather not know.
I'm branded with words I try to overthrow,
Your death, my love, and that of our line, our stock.
Both of our boys are to die whilst in their prime,
One on the battlefield, mere carrion for the dark flock,
The youngest, he says, will die with his head on the block.
And our good name shall be trampled into the grime.
To quell his obscenities I raise my gloved hand,
And screaming thrust my blade through his pale grief.
I slash, lunge and hack to fulfil my Lord's demands
But my point merely rips a gash in his sleeve.
Spreading wide his arms, he shows me his palms,
Then leaps from the cliff to plunge through space
To vanish into the spray of the River Conwy.
No mangled corpse struck the rocks with terrible haste,
But I watched a dove gently glide through the lace
Of the falls, and fly on into the forest's darkening face.

The Gift

for P.A. Morbid

*A poet becomes then an antenna capturing the voices of the world, a
medium expressing his own subconscious and the collective
subconscious. For one moment he possesses wealth usually inaccessible
to him, and then loses it when that moment is over*

                                                    Anna Swir

From the top of the tower the whole town
Is a smouldering fire
Glittering, living embers
Spreading from the riverbanks

Sparks and the odd stray flash of convergence
From up here it's at least
Something that can wear a name
Something to warm your hands on

And feel that maybe you're just beyond its reach
Standing firmly planted
Testing Will against the wind
And turning inanimate

Above the wash of the rush-hour gridlock
I steel myself to know
I can step behind the veil
And mutate into rainfall

Distance is the key to my disorder
Unlike medication
In distance the present ebbs
Voices from the past will speak

Lines of poetry like migrating geese
Cut the evening sky
Their gobble racket gabble
Is a rising tide of song

That floods my gristled mind to breaking point
My arms are laced with scars
The scored skin of angel script
From so many years of letting

The language out in drips of bright berries
A rhythm of red dawnings
Pigeon days and bin bag nights
Of wondering through the streets

Struggling to dampen the intrusions
With ink. How would you cope?
If everything you saw insists
On recounting its story

Climbing plant, brick, leather, cloth and feather
I used to work on pages
And loose leaf sheets
Trying to get it all down

Until I drowned in an ocean of notes
I used a computer
Scrawled on the walls of my room
Sprayed tags over the bridges

A cobweb of symbols in the alleys
Chalk patterns on pavements
On the tiles of the subways
Renaming the town – Babel

I recited my rambles for the crowds
Of starlings circling
Over the allotment's bridge
To all the passing freight trains

Strung up some well hung words as exhibits
On literary nights
At gigs and at festivals
Where my words became solid

I would never remember anything
From opening my mouth
Until waking next morning
In a police station cell

After dreams of being encased in oak
Bubbles of rising sap
Vegetable murmurings
Welling from within my rings

Memory drawn up through a long taproot:
Bonfires on the hillside
Clamour of horns and sirens
A hunt's smear on iron ore

But people said I read with passion
Transforming before them
Leading them away with me
To places beyond their lives

I can't figure out what's mine, what's not
The world speaks through my lips
Though no one calls me prophet
Just a monster on a tower

Sickle-sharp moon, read the text on my arms
We've been mates for as long
As I can remember – Bone Girl
Edit me, be my cold witness

This time I entered life reluctantly
Clinging to the womb walls
Resisting each contraction
Fighting for days from my cave

The tug of Annwn too strong and too sweet
To let go of and slip
Into the realm of edges
A world of sharp corners

All the while she cried and groaned, moaned and wailed
Until his decision.
When I heard it I shivered;
His voice heard over her heart

That slowed to an easy state of dreaming.
What do sleeping hearts dream?
She no longer cried in pain,
But the heart sang of yearning

To hold, protect and kiss her new-born babe
A song of the Outside,
With words like Sun, Wind, Rain, Skin,
Words that taste of chocolate

Then the womb-world split on a scalpel's edge
And Summer flooded in
Gloved fingers, and I'm lifted,
Purple clot into the air

In the fox headed houses off Cannon Street
I dreamed of Welsh valleys
Mountain steams and ragged peaks
Though I've never been to Wales

In the roar of the crowds from Ayresome Park
I heard shields clash, swords ring
The charge of horses, falling men
And the boom of the high falls

While the interview panel enquired
Why do you want this post,
What can you bring to the job?
The patterns of streaming rain

Down the window pane blathered out their trip
The grain of the table
Swirled in a script I could read,
Of growth, storms, the axe and saw

Tick the box beside unemployable
You'd recommend treatment
There being no call these days
For oracles or for seers

He has the Gift, my Aunt Bethan once said
To my mother after
I'd slept the night at her house
You saw Albert, didn't you?

The old man wearing slippers who just walks
Straight through the bedroom wall?
Don't worry he means no harm.
I'd seen him, and a lot more

Although you are little, you are gifted
She said *A gift from the seas*
And from roots of the hills,
And from the depths of rivers

She was a strange old fish my Aunt Bethan
Weak and small as I was,
A virtue lay in my mouth
Ask, whether moon, man or spirit

Her father, she said, had come from Gwynedd
And carried his homeland
Like a pearl behind his grin
When he arrived looking for work

Under the soot filled skies of Middlesbrough
A tall man with the Gift
Of speaking to the spirits
Of seeing through the veil

Though he kept it secret except when pissed
When his eyes would roll back
He would begin to ramble
And end up throwing a fit

Thrash around like a serpent on the ground
His skin changing colour
Hardening to a dark crust
Blue lips sipping forked portents

That's how, she said, *he changed into a god.*
In the midst of a fit
Toward the end of his shift
Slipped through a skin of wet steel

She woke with a pearl tucked under her tongue
In the dream of living
The past coming and going
Open wide, she said, *don't swallow.*

So when the present coils itself too tight
I climb up the tower
To howl, growl and to blubber
To show the pearl in my mouth

To the Bone Girl in the sky, to transmute
To throw off my shoulders
Heave off the sack of my skin
And travel as a shadow

A rogue typo in the text of the town
A semiotic surge
A loose spanner in the works
A stone thrown in a glass-house.

Like the Last Bard

I dunno how you could. I can't even eat normal frigging mushies.
They taste like dead things.

Do 'em in tea, with loads of sugar.

Mank!

But it's like your first ever pint. It's that close to sex.

I'll stick to lager.

I've never felt so connected.
Like nothing can phaze me. Like even that dickhead
Bouncer staring us out in there. I just smiled
And he became a little lamb.

I'll stick with lager.

And there's all this space and space in time.
It's weird and beautiful.

I'll stick with lager. You're just luvved up.
TAXI!

Look at the way the tower's lit up.
It's pouring a rainbow over the town.
So cool and calming you could drink it.

You're off yer head you are!
Jesus.

And the lights from the takeaways on the wet road
Like a magic river that could take us anywhere.

But there's sommat else up there. Sommat's moving.
Look.
Where?

On top of the tower.
Maybe a father for justice with a banner.

Maybe a student protesting against tuition fees
Or the war or sommat.

Naa, it's an old bloke, that is.
Look at his beard, it looks like a sail.

Maybe it's Santa.

Maybe it's the ancient mariner.

The ancient who?

The ancient mariner.

Who's that then?

Some fella in a poem my Nana used to tell.
He wore a dead albatross round his neck.

Like feathered bling? ... So why'd he wear an albatross?

Cos he shot it and was cursed
All of his shipmates came back as zombies.

Zombies! I hate zombies. I always had dreams about em.

Yeah, imagine them all over town, trying to eat yer brains.
Brains. Brains! Brains!

Oh, all over the Hill Street and Captain Cook's square.
Loitering outside of Virgin with Thriller playing in the background.

Never mind that. That's Auld Wanley that, I'd put money on it.

Where?

That divvy up there.

Auld Wanley?

Auld Wanley!

Auld Wanley? The old bloke who shoots his mouth off
on the bandstand every Sunday after a skinful.

Looks like Osama Bin Laden in a crumpled mac.

I know him. Been around for donkeys he has.
Used to see him on the 136 to Billingham
Whenever I slept at me Nana's as a kid.

Osama Bin Laden?

Auld Wanley, you divvy.
Wasn't he a poet or sommat?

He's not a fucking poet. He's a drunk tramp
Frothing at the mouth.

I remember once with me Nana going to town
He was sat opposite staring into space
Muttering to himself and writing in a notebook
with a Ladbrooks pen.

That doesn't mean he's a poet. Means he's off his napper.

I know, but it freaked me out. I thought
He was making spells.

Maybe he's making one now?
I asked me Nan and she shushed me up
Till he got off at Snowdon Road.
Then she told me he was almost famous.

Famous?

Yep.

Fuck off!

Honest. She told me he used to perform at all these events,
Like, hundreds went to em.

What events? When?

Poetry events. When he was young.
Me Nan went to some and they were great she reckons.

Poetry! You taking the piss?

Naa. I'm just telling you what she told me.
She said poetry was a big thing in town in those days.
She was into all that like.

How come?

Used to say that without a story, a song or a poem
You didn't know who you were or where to belong.
Was always banging on about culture and arguing
About politics with our Dad. Used to say he'd sold out.

He's alright your Dad.

But me Nan was a bit of a rebel in her time
And our Dad's always played it safe.

But he makes good money, got a good car
What's her problem?

He's a really good drawer our Dad.
Always said he was wasted in insurance.
Used to have right barnies about it.
Said he should have followed his dreams
Gone to Art College. Dad said that was her dreams though
Not his.

So what happened to Auld Wanley?
How come he didn't make the big time
Became the bandstand king living on a shoe string?
And ends up here on top of the tower?

Dunno.

Do you think he's gonna jump?

Dunno.
In a minute? In an hour?

Dunno.

Maybe he's gonna be up there forever.

Yeah, people'll come from all over to see him.

From Redcar, from Seaton Carew.
From America, from Peru.

They'll take photos, paint him, put him in art galleries.

Reminds me of another poem me Nana used to read.
The Bard. About the last Welsh Warrior Poet
To be hunted down by English troops.

Why?

For keeping the language alive
For not letting anyone forget who they were
For keeping the resistance going
And it all ends up on this cliff over a waterfall
With the soldiers way below riding up to get him.
I can hear her voice.

Yer Nana's dead.

I can hear it. I bet he can too.

Yer off yer head, you.

No, man, listen… he jumps off the cliff just before they get him.

Like Butch and Sundance.

Shall we wait to see if he jumps then
Or call a copper or sommat?

Dunno. It's freezing. Dooya fancy a Big Mac
Before we jump in a cab?

Too right! It's Baltic.
I fancy chicken Mcnuggets and fries, me.

Suomi
& Other Yoiking Locations

Translation

With the taste of Baltic salt on the lips
after barbecue and beers in the woods
we sit and share poetry around the table
try our hands at carrying over meaning.

Much later on the beach with plastic cups
of Bourbon we share smokes, watch the waves.
You should come in Winter, the Finns tell us.

Each year Kalle swims in the frozen sea, Ville too.
Then sauna, then back out to sit in the snow.
Feel your heart beat slow right down.
Feel your energy levels fall. Its better
than drugs, sex and rock and roll.

These maniacs have about thirty names for snow
and *Ensilumi* is my favourite, the winter's
first attempts at a tentative illumination.

The City with the Beautiful Far Away Mind

I climb the old wooden roller coaster
on Linnanmaki. Cool wind, clear night.
A few hours before the dawn even the harbour
is asleep, though Suomelina's ever watchful
of the sea and the land, the White Palace is snoring,
as I edge along a joist and squeeze quietly onto the tracks.
Inertia binds this fun park. The stalls, bars and booths
are padlocked and shuttered. The Waltzers and T-pots
are dreaming, The Big Wheel cradles its cages.
The Hall of Mirrors is locked up like a multiform freak
to gaze endlessly into itself. No security
nor guard dogs nor cctv, so I walk the steep slope
of the first big drop, imagining thousands of screams
falling like dead leaves tumbling down the rocks
to the city below, becoming snagged in the fence
or the tangle of bushes, stepped on, rained on
and buried by the first snows of the season.
The city is lit up now, twinkling, its limits
defined by black forest, black sea.
The drinkers and dancers have spilled, sweaty
from the night clubs, eaten at a grilli and ambled
homeward to peel off their layers and fall
into fucking then sleeping. Somewhere
down there Satu feels a kick, wakes with a craving
for a reindeer steak, her child swims,
turns and makes her breasts ache.
The semi-pro wrestler who wants to defend his nation
from immigrants, and played his air guitar
on stage in The Rock to Bohemian Rhapsody
now sits in a chair splashed by lamplight sighing,
suppressing homo-erotic impulses by leafing
through a porn mag before hitting the sack.

The retired history teacher with his home counties accent,
who bought me a Salmiakki in the karaoke bar,
collapses drunk on his single bed. He will dream sporadically
until eight of Andy Cap fighting in the Winter War with Flo.
In the cobbled square two policemen are trying to flush
a human spider out of the bus shelter and into their van.
He has taken to moving on all fours, arched in a crab
his eyes wild through the strands of his long lank hair,
while his mouth is moving, chewing, only a wordless
mewling emerges. He has lost all of his words
with his bus fare down the drain, where they echo
to him through the dripping sewers. On the top
of the roller coaster I smoke a cigarette, then sit very still,
watching for the advance of winter, wondering
if I'll remember the way back to the apartment,
feeling the pulse of the slumbering, restless city
through the planks of old timber. I suspect I could fly
but know its a long way down to the ground from here,
the drops are steep, I'll need to step with care and realise
with a shiver it's high time I submitted to gravity,
let the night and all of its lightness pass, time
to pull myself together and find a bed to fall into.

Wildlife

On the island of Vepsa there's a midsummer-pole
two couples are training for the Wife Carrying Race
there are also pike in the reeds. Jenni knows it.
They're calling her name. *Haukio, O' Haukio*
but she's doing her best to ignore them
and points out an oyster catcher
darting from the Laituri; completely unaware
that it was recently voted the nation's
most beautiful bird and awarded a brand new name
which no one seems to remember

On a granite snub on the island of Vepsa
we build a fire, uncork bottles, spread out
the picnic, talk about style, rhyme, language
heat seeking elk flies, bears and Bukowski.
We've been drinking for days and not sleeping
having discovered how sauna tricks the mind
and body into believing otherwise

In perpetual sunlight hallucinations
are a regular occurrence. The islands are still rivets
in the iron sea, but they could turn at any moment.
The wildlife knows how to live by extremes.
There are Thunder Gods here and rumours of fish queens.

In The Shaman's Garden

We were trying hard to admire
Alpo Jaakola's sacred sculptures
but the forest mosquitoes
had their own cow in the gutter.
They sent us shuddering and slapping
between lines of pines, splashes
of silver birch, papery peeling ghosts
with knots as bruises and troll-scratched eyes.

I stepped through the hole of the Shaman's Shadow
into a loganberry glade. In the circle of Gods
snakes eat their tails. The Field-Maker sits
on a crumbling throne pointing at a piece
called *Memory of the Dead*. Or was it
The 2nd Stuttering of the Flesh?

Unaware that in a ward across the two-hour
time-zone of thirty thousand islands, my grandmother
breathed, breathed, breathed, then didn't
so my parents and uncle could sigh in relief.

Web Slinging

for Lorna Drinkwater

Desperate for time alone to mourn
I drink koskenkorva moonshine
with my name on the bottle
on the bank of the River Aura
after a night of Thrash Metal.

On the bridge the early-men
fish for gates, haul them up
and lay them out to dry, as I
dredge for memories of my Gran

beyond the paper-thin suffering
of the last visits to the hospital.
The life-lights leaving in stages
and her pleading for peace.

I was casting for other stuff:
making paper-chains, Christmas crackers,
holding scissors, folding edges
and the way she could draw;

taught me to mark, shade, cross-hatch
and begin to see the shapes of things
with sparkling eyes and talk of books.

The *Amazing Spiderman* comics on Thursdays,
and how she perfected the art
of incessant chatter.
Talk to any bugger she will.

And how she could flirt,
broke a string of hearts and engagements
and my heart too, when I was twelve
and saw a hand-tinted photo of her at twenty one.

Funny Bloody Woman
who sang of setting the world on fire
while making Sunday dinner.

Other recollections swarmed, rushed through
my quivering threads but most refused to stick.

Off it, doesn't come close
once koskenkorva kicks-in
and I end up blubbering, scaling a crane
like Peter Parker trying to touch the sun.

Some Bad Hat

In Little Valhalla
the Lionman said (in English)
that he really liked my hat.
His eyes and smile widened
with appreciation as he asked
Where might I buy a hat like that?
He'd once tried one on in Denmark,
but didn't buy it, and now seeing the way
that it sat on my head, how the rim
cast a slight shadow over my eyes,
he says he wishes that he had.
I told him I'd bought it in a shop
on the shore of Loch Ness,
which made him sigh *No!*
and shake his mane.
Would you like to try it on?
He seemed honoured, handled it gently,
slid it on and turned to his girlfriend
who said something which pleased him.
Her mother, who was the spit
of Thing One (or was it Thing Two?),
was impressed by the look,
she wanted to be the Cat in my Hat
and asked if she might try it too.
Once on she announced to the bar
how it felt *So right! So right!*
and how she had never been one
to wear, in the past, anything
like a cowboy hat, but this,
this was something special.
So we all drank to The Hat
and ordered another bottle,
then we yoiked the hat's
reluctant return to my head,
and now and again Lionman
would glance over, grin,

with a glint in his eye and say
Nice fucking hat! Then my mobile
bleeped with the arrival of a text.
I fished it out and read,
Cum to the toilets, there's
something weird going on. Kalle.
I looked at Kalle across the table,
made my way to the toilet
where he joined me to say
he'd just overheard the Lionman
say, in Finnish, to his girl,
They are just to my taste.
We should invite them back.
The one with the hat
thinks he is invincible
and it would be fun to wake them
with a big surprise.
But the girl and her mum were
against the idea and Lionman
was getting quite upset.
Kalle advised we be careful,
accept no invitations or drinks,
so we finished our bottle,
said our goodbyes and left
with a wave and a nod
to a roar of pure longing,
Nice Fucking Hat!
Nice Fucking Hat!
Nice Fucking Hat!

Scales

For Jenni Haukio

The girl
from the islands
gave me a strip of cured
fish skin, slightly larger than
my palm. Crispy and translucent
when held to the light, like a page from
Poseidon's bible, a patch from a mermaid's
cape. 'It's made,' she said, 'from the kind of fish
legged men can only catch through the Winter
by breaking the Baltic ice and lowering
a line into the depths through the hole.
All through the Summer they lie
at the bottom cold and still
like the hands of
the drowned.'

Hung Over Voipalla

The drooping birch trees
against the night's cloudless sky
are wrought iron gallows
heavy with chains.

Around the roots
a century of dead dandelion heads
reach for a wind strong enough
to stir their future resurrection.

Homesick, I hang in the company
of a carved crow totem, in the heady
scent of lilac blossom torches
surrounding the sculpture garden.

We've planned to go fishing tomorrow
after digging for worms, but as always
time slips its chains on the birches
and floats away like seeds on the breeze.

Maybe the Grey Man

What do you make of the quiet man who stalks
the pavements to the harbour with determined tortoise steps,
as if each stone was the unbroken shell of a quail's egg?
And every other Wednesday rides the trams to the market place
to buy two bunches of bright chrysanthemums to decorate
his window sill; and because it's rude to stare you watch him
unfocussed, weaving through the peripheries of busy crowds,
wondering – was it an industrial accident or some sort of disease
that washed out all his colour, left him living gunmetal grey?

If you should see the grey man, never look at him straight.
Glance the other way, don't tempt fate.
Resist the urge to gaze directly in his face.
Didn't Mommy ever warn you of changes in the wind?

Ignore his ashen clothes, the heavy duty charcoal jacket,
those shining strands of silver hair that sweep his pewter brow?
Don't gawp like a gutted cod at his cheeks of pinched permafrost,
but glance, glance the other way, at the floor and back again.
Don't watch the puckering oyster fringe of his reticent lips
as he leans in close to converse with the florist, beware
the burst of his rain clouds, drifting wafts of woodsmoke
under the peak of his cap, pulled low.

If you should spot the grey man, never look at him straight.
Glance the other way, step aside, or wait.
Resist the temptation to stop and shake his hand.
Didn't Mommy ever warn you of changes in the wind?

It seems like no one's noticed he lives in a perpetual shadow
that tinges everything he touches a definite shade of taupe.
Though you've overheard a rumour he's the last forest troll;
a changeling swapped in the cradle for a pink cheeked boy
with wide blue eyes and rose hip lips, who slept by an open window
at the forest's edge. He dreams in fossils of his human double,
living the life of a wood sprite under the roots of an ancient tree
growing on the crown of a sacred mound, no human's ever seen.

If you should meet the grey man, never look at him straight.
Glance the other way, don't stop to speak a word.
Resist the sudden urge to follow in his wake.
Didn't Mommy ever warn you of changes in the wind?

And didn't someone mention, he's coated in a fine growth of lichen
from sitting on a rock some forty eight hours a week,
watching the steel-tinted waves lap at his webbed feet?
Perhaps it's a self induced psychosomatic condition,
stemming from the day he discovered his soul mate's affair
and everything around him turned harsh survival slate.
He's since become a living glass of lonkero – the perfect hangover drink
his skin's not skin at all, but grapefruit and gin, and if you'd dare
to touch him, your fingers would slip through liquid
far enough in to tap the ice cube of his heart
that refuses to thaw in the Midsummer heat.

If you should spot the grey man, never look at him straight
Don't stroke his cat fish whiskers or tickle his scales
Or catch the scent of his flowers, don't take the bait.
Didn't Mommy ever warn you of changes in the wind?

Lovi

On Interviewing Esa Hirvonen

Jesus of the Elk writes as a matter of personal survival.
His poems are tracks through snow covered woods;
a tuft of coarse hair snagged on a barbed wire brier,
burnt wood, cigarette butts.

They lead to places I'd rather not visit,
through brambles, hazels and junipers
to the banks of a black river.

He writes to get at the truth of things.
Singing the origins, like a brooding enchanter –
Vainamoinen; tired from freezing lakes
of moving mountains by hammering out
the beat of words from inside the belly of a giant.

But palindromes, he says,
allow me to play. They lighten my mind.

After talking with Jesus of the Elk
on the banks of a black river;
with the music of the dead
drifting over the water from the stereo
in their summer house, my instinct
is to spit in his face. I want to slide a spear
into the side of this gentle creature, though
I call him friend and I'm not a violent man.

But he leaves me shambling and convinced
that we all exist as Nobody inside the Cyclops' gut,
sometimes peering out of its fundamental eye
at a world without perspective. Scrabbling
for three lost words to release us,
and complete The Song of our Ship,
give it the spirit to cradle us
as we continue our voyage home.

Home

I'm wondering why
a grown man would weep
a large, but solitary tear from one eye,
without the shudder of a single sob
as he lies in his own bed after a long trip,
stumbling through the many faces
of an unfamiliar language,
following the long white lines
of roads through a shrinking forest;
now of all times, with the full weight
and warmth of his lover's leg sleeping
over his own, and the shallow, steady rise
and fall of a breath on his cheek.

Paddling in Staithes

I: NOTICE:

When paddling
every time clouds pass around your ankles
the seagulls burst out laughing.

II: Testing the water

The pool has gone completely since the improvements;
it left with the tankers that brought the sea brace
and saved Bottom End from drowning.

The man with the load on his shoulder
is the last long-line fisherman in the village.
The guy with silver hair, real tan and a frown
is the fishing inspector from Scar to Sunder.

And although some questions raise eyebrows,
(about the lifeboat, the choir, the cobbles, the parking),
it's the first good day of the year for sitting,
drinking coffee, for staring out to sea like a pillar of salt.

For braving the shallows of the bay
and gasping at the shock of its nip on bare skin
while disturbing the surface and the silt
and the village's inverted twin, with each numb step.

For a spot of time-travelling through Steers
on the beck's flow of barely prompted yarns,
through eyes peering inward like a holiday home's window
into closets stuffed with memorabilia: a laugh, a sigh,

a rennie's sly smile, through all of the synonyms for swine,
never knitting or sewing after 6 o'clock
nor baiting lines nor potting of a Friday,
and every woman in a bonnet is your Aunt.

Paddle around the grin at a cuff about the ear,
head in your hands and playing with your brains
for a fall on the mat with one foot in the custard.
Hear a ringer's bare feet pad over the eaves,

shuffle the viaduct's girders to the pigeon nests beneath.
Milkshake bubbles blown for the Beatles' Grinkle visit
burst to a petticoat's swish, the stilettos' click
polished for the biker boys riding in from the Boro.

Enter on a lost half crown – found a year later,
or two prize-winning gooseberries the size of hen's eggs.

III: Sandfly

Severe. You'd be hit with a stick oft' enough.
Is all George answers to the question of the past.
From his chin, hard as a lobster shell, hangs a classic
Steers stand off, and I am but a sandfly resting on a fossil.
Today the lingo of flying bugs escapes him,
as he's intent on steering us through the sea's slow grind,
navigating time, biting further into Cowbar with each new tide.

IV: Dinosaur

The Old Nab is a sheer grimace
at the encroaching sea.
Hidden from the view of walkers
on the Cleveland Way
by folding fields at the foot
of Quarry Bank, where, some days
on mornings such as these,
a German plane limps out of memory
over the piers, up Gunn Gutter
and over the head of Dick Porrit, standing
shouting, *Al a pot tha', Jerry, al a pot tha!*
to crash and litter the bank
with twisted steel and precious scrap.

Old Nab squats, a snub at waves and sky
hoarding its rumoured seam of jet
and watching like it always has
for Viking longships
Spanish galleons running before a storm
German battleships in the fog
and the diminishing fleet of Steers cobles
coming and going on the edge of extinction.

V

Threatened Village: the storm of '53

based on a painting by Lillian Colbourne

Ghost tales are hard to come by in a village
so rooted in its rich and colourful practicality,
but I'm shown a painting, full of spectres – djinns
masquerading as spume, devouring the slip,
climbing the gables, flooding bedrooms
and hurling The Star of Hope end over end.

Whitewash thick as the weather, so that all boundaries
are lost between people and place, a past and its future.
Is that Aunt Parky's piano floundering under the bridge?
Are those coffins turning in the swollen beck?
Are those people climbing onto rooftops,
smudges scaling the cliff? Are those marks railings
or the ribs of a whale? No matter, hold on to them tight
or else the gale will sweep you beyond anyone's reach.

The Great Entertainer

Hartlepool 9 February 1861

for two days and two nights he had the sea fight the sky
the coastline was whipped between iced wind and high tide
and cracked like a mast

the ships were their tops
spun onto the fangs of Longscar Rocks
or rolled up by the gale's head straight into the pier

one into the next they wracked up their scores
twentythirtyfortyfiftysixtyseventyeightymore

first light, next morning, those who'd seen the show
picked the reshaped beach with the vacant eyes of fish
as cobles struck out

for the first catch in days
combers salvaged wrecks and wheeled the drowned
to their house, and the weepers just stood, staring

at the breakers; at the Elephant Rock, looking docile
sleeping off their tempers. The Block Sands was a bill-poster
signed by the great entertainer:

The World Famous Widow-Maker
& His Zinc Lined Cabinet of Death

and the lifeboat crews
oar sore and storm deaf, swore they'd heard a Waff's song
from the holes of Fairy Cove; foretelling the fate

of the Rising Sun and all but one aboard her
lucky Henry Prosser, poor little Henry Prosser.

Ritual

Old Blakey looks like he's lived in Heretu forever
as he squats on Fish Sands at the foot of the steps
in bicycle clips and Lieutenant Columbo's mac
his iron aged bike leans against the south sea wall.

He takes out a powder blue dustpan and brush
sets to dusting the beach into a Lidl carrier bag.
Leaves a neat two-foot square of flattened beige
with bristled plough-lines like a garden in Kyoto.

Climbs up the steps with his bag quarter full
mounts the bike and peddles past the Pot House,
to sit at home and sift for the tide's favourite grain
the beautiful one; the one with the World in.

Peripheries

The lure of the landscape
with summits banging like fireworks
makes driving a danger
along the single-track road

but the corner of my eye
snags the outline of a hooded crow
perched on a boulder
and part of the same note.

It's staring across Kilfinichen Bay
from the land that time forgot
or at least mislaid somewhere
in an instant of absent mindedness.

Its eyes are locked on Iona;
the rain clouds muffling the peaks
contemplating patience, unruly
precision, in the dialect of mountains.

Its head is cocked for an eagle's cry
a small rodent's rustle in heather
and the sudden, rare scent of a roadkill.
Its beak has stripped the bones of touring voles

Bedraggled monks and would-be-saints
that have trod the way
in haar, swirling snow and ever-shifting light.
I slow and steer into a passing place

Let a tour bus lumber by
the driver lifts his finger; his cargo
of kilted Canadians, discovering roots
watch too, as the crow-stone splits

wing tips beat the brimming shore
as if it's bang out of order. Rising over
the remains of an abandoned fishing boat;
dragging the eye, and more, effortlessly
up the cliff face of Armeanach.

Whorling

Helmsley Moor 2005

Reaching the Great Boulder the kids
climb and squat to survey the empty world's
burnt heather and bald spots; slumbering rocks
sunk in peat, miscellaneous cairns, withered
milestones marking the moortop's crew cut.
Its remoteness unnerves them.
Rain, then sun, then shade follow warm wafts
rising from the dale like curlews bubbling
through a heat haze, gliding over bracken.
The sky bruises to blood orange over Bilsdale,
with hours left till sunset. *I could die up here!*
Someone whispers, *I'd just die.*

The boulder is a patchwork of lichen,
dried chewy on a playground bench.
Its surface eroded into a lattice of runnels,
deep as a man's hand, where millipedes
pour themselves in orange-umber undulations
from one shade to another, disturbed by the chatter
of these bipeds from the pavements.

We ask for a mere 60 seconds of silence.
I give the word and the children fall into the upland quiet,
listen to the boulder breathing, the moortop moving,
the sky racing itself and self burning away like heather
across the ridge, along the road-winding river
into the trees, the snow-melt on the boulder
filling the runnels of scars, brimming over the whorling
bowls of ourselves like the bubbling calls of curlews.

A minute passes and no one's willing to break the spell.
They grant this world an age of thirty seconds more before
Kurt asks quietly, as if he's in church, *Is it okay to speak now?*
Course it is, someone says, as a cloud
the shape of a millipede rolls up the sun.

Pilililu

Every force evolves a form
while this thing lasted
it was pure and very strong.

Hugh MacDiarmid – Island Funeral

Such a ruin emanates – something,
sends my nerve ends atingle,
high above the now tended plain
and the peat bog of Moine Mhor
Gaelic kings were crowned,
the Stone rang its human cry
through this Valley of Ghosts,
over cairns, circles, fairy mounds
out to the shrouded islands.

Grass grows over the abandoned fort,
the forgotten forge, stables, well,
the rough royal chambers softening
edges to rolling suggestions.
You say, *This place is charged*,
brings you close to tears, while
my body expands: my skin a sail,
my spine a mast, my rib cage
a coracle frame, navigating
a winding stretch of river
to the sounds of the eternal sea.

The split stone of Dunnad's throne
sings pilililui pilililui pilililui as lives
and cultures come and go, like tides,
we both know we've been here before
as fish, fox, red deer, wild boar,
and one day will come again,
each of us bearing a different name.

Running 2000

Running the gauntlet of the roman road past the college
disturbing a box-sniffing terrier on a dropped slice of pizza
in a squashed Manhattan box, still displaying the skyline
just as it was, head afloat with a traveller's tales of Haiti
stripping down the deceits of interest free Bohemia;
with poverty, war-talk & the day of reckoning
looming over a bed warmed by love in the Little Houses
by the Water snoring stars out bright no moon nor wind
nor snow but the always orange haze of streetlights
swilling half-way up the basin, fireworks finally fading,
festive lights twinkling & the pretty pink neons
aglow on Centre North East like Jacob's Ladder got him
mulling over Bernicia & all the feudal lines drawn up
between the Tees & the Tyne, the Wear & the Tweed
the Prince Bishopdom, the Dane-law, De Brus' estates
the precious shifts in vowel sounds, inherited battlegrounds
& sweet Lucia de Thweng in a secret castle out by Skelton,
the maccam's yards & all those mines of ransacked ore;
then foot-stumbling as if caught on the chin by St Hilda
first facing the Headland with a stiff upper lip
or Oswy's cuff while considering the potential lineage
of kingship; at the cemetery gates he was hailed
by a Mohawk brave and a tribe of stillborn babes
recently remembered in stone, saw the Quakers of Port Darlo'
moving themselves into new plots overnight;
was reminded momentarily of Bosnia Hergovinia
the warring maps of mis-matched histories; a sharp flash
of film footage of a man running naked from a bomb-shelled
farmfull & Daniel from the corner, his Mam & Dad
trying asylum in the Boro & unavoidably thought up
the mind-bite of two crumbling towers: Ever Falling
thoughts about how it felt this passed year for those
with an ear to the ground like things were happening here
like this town was going places: Paris Milan Ground Zero
Sarajevo Baghdad The Great Land of Leather PC World

wherever whenever & for how long no one can say
because it's never what you expect it to be this town's
not what you project then he's thinking of The Faraway Tree
& it seems a suitable analogy for a town off the cuff –
too used to making itself up to reply to the rhetoric
of so *whoo dooya wannabe* with anything more
than a cynical shrug (*inshallah*) with the river turning
tricks across the width of the basin changing course
& claiming old debts: Jack's Victoria Cross
the pocket Bible of an unknown soldier souvenir
postcards from Cork a shotgun in a sportsbag a book
of love poems from the Punjab, pouring the Good & the Bad
between unflinching Gares into breakers struggling
to believe in the past of a future geography we might
peg a hope on this New Year's Eve that despite & because
of it all's as soft and shiny as a park mallard's wing.

Tracking Samhain

in Cabanas

The breeze is peppered,
brings the edge of All Saints
trailing on the hem
of a day of heavy rain.
It rushes through clusters of bushes
whose roots grow deep in sandy soil.

Small clouds punctuate the sky –
streaked in a riot of pomegranate
split by time,
dropping a shower of seeds
in sweet pink flesh, with the promise
of a fine day tomorrow.

At the sand's edge
you can dig for bait,
bent double and lumber
like the others
that dot the low tide line,
scraping wet furrows, cast
a shadow the shape of a camel.

You can write your name
with your hand held like a cup
or rake, or watch
the young man
handle the rowing boat, checking
his father's lines and pots in the lagoon.

You could follow the prints
of a mammal,
perhaps a wild cat,
up the slope into the dunes,
its dance steps trotting between
a full stomach, the edge of hunger.

Sharp claws mark the way
through the dark of beached boats
clumps of grasses;
slinking sometime ahead
nose windward, reading its script,
with the tell-tale base-note of a run-away.

A beggar prince working-out
its bearings between the surf
trying to level
the sandbank,
the constellation of the fishing village;
where eldest daughters close gift shops

Lock up silver Buddhas,
black cockerels, bells;
as seasoned sweethearts
serve espresso
behind snack bars of sugar coated cakes.

Where a sad-eyed tourist on a well-earned
veranda peels an apple
in front of a mirror,
humming to the tune of an insect
that uses its shell as a jembe.

Snatches of their song drift Spainward.
I don't care if you're wrong.
I do not care if you are wrong.
It's only a matter of time.

Here Be Monsters

I've been searching for an island called Ishmael
with a habit of falling off the map.
where, it's said, a white hart darts like light
through thickets, bounds through the line
where Earth meets sky; leaves you winded
by a scent you've known,
but never pinned down with a name.

I remember the old girl asking,
– *Where've yous been?*
– *Out looking for a worm.*
– *A worm?*
– *The Sockburn Worm.*
– *What's that?*
– *A dragon that was once slain just up the river,
  and buried under a boulder.*
– *You mean to tell me, you've had that poor bairn
  traipsing through the muddy fields
  on a Boxing Day as bitter as this?*
– *Yeah, didn't find it though.*
– *Bloody Fool!*
She shuddered to her bones.

I'm after a barren land called Ishmael
with a beach like a stark blank page,
harsh as the first slush of winter.
A non-place of terra potential, pure borderdom,
without so-much as a sign saying 'Ultimate Thule'.

I have no harpoon, no Conyers Falchion,
so I'll bait a snare, string out a line to catch me a worm
and return under sail filled by its breath.